Contents

The seven-day-old queen	4
A violent land	6
The most perfect child	8
Mary, queen of France	10
Farewell France	12
A disastrous love	14
Murder and treachery	16
A gunpowder plot	18
Marriage to Bothwell	20
The darkest hour	22
Escape to England	24
The Casket Letters	26
Fotheringhay	28
Important dates	30
Glossary	31
Books to read	31
Index	32

The seven-day-old queen

Mary **Stuart**, queen of Scotland, was one of the most remarkable women of her day. Beautiful and extremely charming, she lived through such violent events that her story has fascinated people ever since. Brave and affectionate, she was also disastrously emotional, with tragic consequences.

Mary was born the daughter of King James V of Scotland and his French wife, Mary of Guise. At the time of her birth, in December 1542, Scotland was still separate from England and had its own **monarchy**. Just a few days before her birth, the

A portrait of the young Mary.

Scots suffered a terrible defeat at the battle of Solway Moss. Many were killed by the English forces of King Henry VIII and more than 1,000 Scots noblemen were captured and taken to London.

King James was heartbroken. In despair, he fell ill. Messengers arrived to tell him that the queen, his wife, had given birth to a daughter named Mary. This did nothing to ease his anguish. A few days later, King James died without ever seeing his daughter. As the only **heir to the throne**, Mary was declared queen of Scotland. She was then just one week old.

James V of Scotland and his French wife, Mary of Guise.

Mary Queen of Scots

Dorothy Turner

Illustrations by Martin Salisbury

Great Lives

Available in paperback:

Beethoven
Henry VIII
Mary Queen of Scots
Queen Elizabeth I
Queen Victoria
William Shakespeare

Editor: Alison Millar

First published in 1988 by
Wayland (Publishers) Limited
61 Western Road, Hove
East Sussex BN3 1JD, England

British Library Cataloguing-in-Publication Data
Turner, Dorothy
    Mary Queen of Scots. – (Great lives)
    1. Mary, *Queen of Scots* – Juvenile
    literature. 2. Scotland – Kings and
    rulers–Biography – Juvenile literature
    I. Title   II. Salisbury, Martin   III. Series.
    941.105'092'4   DA 787.A5

120.1
MAR

HARDBACK ISBN 1-85210-175-X

PAPERBACK ISBN 0-7502-1333-7

Phototypeset by Kalligraphics Ltd, Redhill, Surrey
Printed and bound in Italy by G. Canale & C.S.p.A., Turin

0760 213 3337 4209

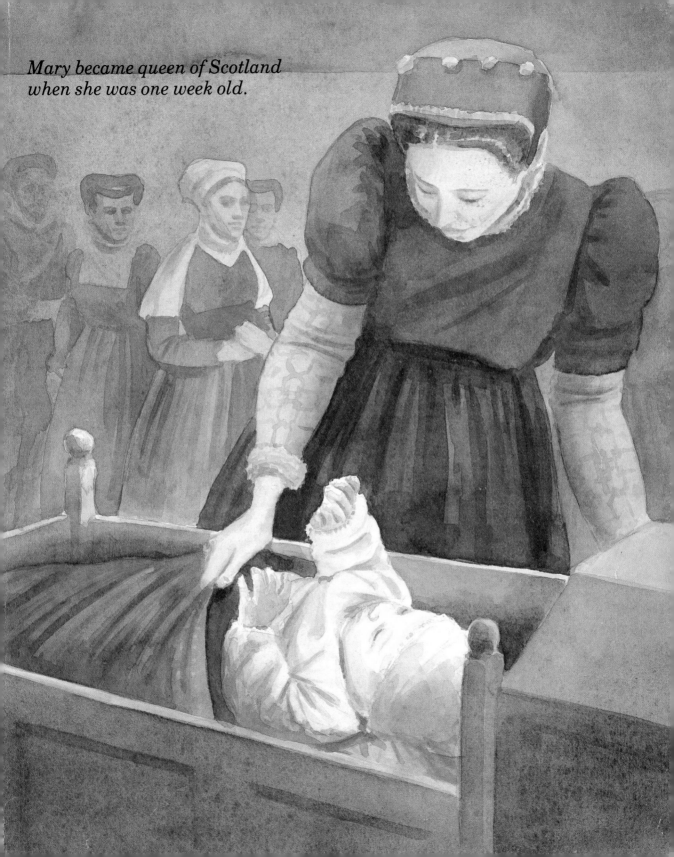

Mary became queen of Scotland
when she was one week old.

A violent land

A marriageable queen (even if she was still a baby) was always a temptation to ambitious men and Henry VIII, king of England, soon saw the opportunity to increase his power in Scotland. In 1543 a **treaty** was drawn up, arranging marriage between Mary and his own son, Prince Edward. (Edward was then six years old; Mary was not yet one.)

Scotland, however, was a country of dangerously divided loyalties. It had a small population, most of whom were desperately poor. The lords of the land were endlessly involved in family feuds and rivalries. Violence and lawlessness were common. Scottish **Catholics** hated the idea of their queen marrying a **Protestant** Englishman. Instead they looked to France for help.

In this explosive situation Mary was in peril, so she and her mother were hurried to the safety of Stirling Castle. Here the nine-month-old baby Mary was crowned queen.

The five-year-old Mary was taken to France in 1548.

Above *Stirling Castle, where the infant Mary was hidden.*

Below *Edward VI. His father Henry VIII of England wished him to marry Mary.*

Throughout her early childhood, the English continued to try to subdue Scotland. On 10 September 1547, English and Scots met again at the Battle of Pinkie Cleugh. It was another disaster for the Scots. Mary was hidden from danger in an ancient priory on Inchmahome, a tiny island on a lake.

It became clear that Mary was not safe in Scotland, so the Scottish Parliament gave its consent for her to be taken to France, where she should marry the French king's son. Henry II, King of France, sent his own royal ship to Scotland to collect her. On 29 July 1548, the five-year-old girl said a sad farewell to her mother and set sail for a new life.

The most perfect child

On her arrival in France, everything changed for the better. Instead of the cold, dark castles of Scotland and the constant fear of attack, Mary was now the centre of adoring attention at the luxurious court of the French king. She was clever, charming and pretty. The king said she was 'the most perfect child that I have ever seen'.

Mary quickly learned the new language (after all, her mother was French) and settled into the life of the royal nursery.

When Mary first arrived in France she could only speak English, but she soon learned the French language.

As well as studying Latin, Spanish and Italian, Mary learned to draw, play the lute and to sing and dance while in France.

As the fiancée of the king's eldest son, Francis, she was treated with special reverence.

The royal children travelled constantly from palace to palace, dressed in the finest clothes and with dozens of servants. It seems to have been a time of almost endless happiness. Mary was also well educated. Tutors taught her Latin, Spanish, Italian and some Greek. She learned drawing, music and dancing – at which she excelled.

In 1550, to Mary's great delight, her mother came over from Scotland to be with her for a while. As she grew up, she was daily becoming more French as the memory of the rough days in Scotland faded.

Mary, queen of France

Mary and her fiancé, Francis, had been childhood friends in the royal nursery. Now, as teenagers, they were to become man and wife. Mary had grown tall and beautiful. Francis, however, was a poor weak invalid, physically deformed and painfully shy. He seemed to get on with nobody but Mary, whom he adored. Mary seemed genuinely fond of him.

Mary and Francis were married in 1558 in the Cathedral of Notre Dame in Paris. The whole court rejoiced at the banquet that followed.

On 24 April 1558, Mary (who was then fifteen) and the fourteen-year-old Francis were married. The ceremony, which was magnificent, was followed by banqueting and rejoicing.

A few months later, Mary's cousin, Elizabeth **Tudor**, came to the English throne. As Queen Elizabeth I she was to affect Mary's life tragically, and the

careers of the two queens were always to be contrasted with each other. Elizabeth, cool and politically clever, was never to surrender herself to the domination of a husband, as the headstrong Mary was later to do so disastrously.

To Catholics, however, Mary had a better claim than Elizabeth to the English throne. Henry VIII had divorced his first wife to marry Anne Boleyn, Elizabeth's mother. The Pope never recognized this divorce and so Catholics could not consider Elizabeth, an **illegitimate** child, to be the proper heir to the throne. They felt that Mary, as a direct descendant of Henry VII, had a greater right to rule. The French king, Henry II, even had Mary proclaimed queen of England, Ireland and Scotland. Another title was soon to be hers: In July 1559 Henry II was fatally injured during a tournament. Mary's young husband became King Francis II. At only sixteen years of age, Mary added to her list of titles that of queen of France.

Farewell France

The simple happiness of Mary's French life was now about to end for ever. In June 1560, when she was eighteen-years-old, she heard of her mother's death in Scotland. Mary collapsed with grief.

More sadness followed quickly. Her husband's health deteriorated and within the year he, too, was dead. His mother, Catherine de' Medici, took over the government of the country and Mary was reduced to the status of a mere widow. When her half-brother James Stewart (later called the Earl of Moray) visited her and asked her to

Right *Mary leaves France, never to see it again.*

Below *In 1560 Mary lost both her mother and her husband.*

return to Scotland, Mary agreed.

She did not want to return. Scotland had become very much a Protestant country in the thirteen years of her absence, and a foreign Catholic queen would not be welcome. Those Scots who would support her were often divided among themselves by feuds.

As Mary sailed from Calais, she looked back to the French coastline and said sadly (and correctly): 'Farewell France, farewell. I believe I shall never see you again.'

Ahead of her lay a hostile Scotland and a wary English queen. Elizabeth was alarmed that her cousin – so much more beautiful and charming than she – was returning with a claim to the English throne. This rival would have to be watched.

A disastrous love

Mary landed in Scotland in thick mist. No crowds gathered to greet her and there was no lodging arranged for her. The reception in Edinburgh was warmer, but in effect the country was ruled by the Protestant Church and in particular by a strict, **puritanical** reformer, John Knox.

Mary was everything Knox hated: French, Catholic and a woman. As she settled into Holyrood Palace in Edinburgh, she decorated it in French style and filled it with her courtiers.

John Knox, the Protestant reformer, fiercely opposed Mary's return to Scotland.

She also danced and sang. To Knox, Mary was the Devil. He turned many people against her. Mary, however, disliked religious intolerance and violence. She

Holyrood Palace in Edinburgh was rather a grim home for someone used to the grandeur and gaiety of life at the French court.

wanted her subjects to have a better life, and to be free to choose their religion.

Mary was also a passionate woman and she now made a terrible mistake by falling disastrously in love with her cousin. Henry, Lord Darnley, was tall and handsome and Mary adored him. Unfortunately she failed to see that he was also cruel, ambitious and arrogant.

Despite strong opposition, which brought Scotland to the brink of civil war, Mary and Darnley were married on 29 July 1565. Darnley was a Catholic and the Protestant Scots did not want a Catholic king and queen. Until her marriage, Mary had relied on the advice and support of her half-brother, the Earl of Moray. Now she chose to ignore him and to everyone's dismay, she gave her husband the title King of Scotland.

Mary fell in love with the handsome but arrogant Lord Darnley and they were married in July 1565.

Murder and treachery

Now intrigue was rife, with Protestant lords rebelling against the Catholic queen and eager to take power themselves. Chief among them was the Earl of Moray, who had always wanted to rule Scotland himself and was now very bitter towards Mary.

Some of the lords managed to get the weak Darnley into their power, and they proposed to him a terrible plot. Their hatred was focused on Mary's secretary, an Italian musician called David

Mary's half-brother, the Earl of Moray, turned against her when she married Darnley.

Riccio. On 9 March 1566, as Mary ate supper with Riccio and friends in her room, Darnley entered by his private staircase with another conspirator, a notoriously wicked lord called Ruthven. There were angry words and a struggle. Darnley held Mary back while Ruthven stabbed Riccio. Riccio was dragged from the room and stabbed by the other conspirators repeatedly until he was dead.

Mary faced the murderous scene with great courage. At the time she was six months pregnant. Maybe the murder had been enacted in front of her in the hopes that she would be taken ill from shock and lose the child, and possibly her own life too. Certainly, for the rest of her days Mary believed that Darnley had intended to kill her and their unborn child.

However both Mary and the child survived. On 19 June 1566 the 24-year-old queen gave birth to a healthy son, James.

A gunpowder plot

Now Mary hated Darnley. For support she turned to the chief noble, the Earl of Bothwell, whom she saw as a strong protector. He was also an adventurous and ruthlessly.

In February, 1567, the house where Darnley was staying was blown up. He was found, strangled, in the garden. No one will ever know the part that Mary played in his death.

ambitious man who had been involved in many wild escapades.

Mary had found out the truth about Darnley and regretted marrying him. Others, too, had plans to rid Scotland of the 'young fool and proud tyrant'. Bothwell and his companions had violent and lawless plans.

Mary and Darnley no longer lived together and in the early hours of 10 February 1567, the house in Edinburgh in which Darnley was staying was blown up by a huge explosion. The cellars had been filled with gunpowder. Darnley had managed to escape the explosion by climbing out of a window, but his body was found in the garden, strangled.

Ever since, people have debated just what happened that night and how far Mary knew what Bothwell and the other lords were planning. Nothing can

The Earl of Bothwell who brought about Darnley's death.

be proved, but it seems unlikely that Mary knew of the plot to murder her husband. It was well known that she disliked violence and cruelty. Certainly nothing in her pampered upbringing at the French court had prepared her for the **barbarism** of the land she had come to rule.

19

Marriage to Bothwell

Two months after Darnley's death, Mary made a fateful visit to see her baby son at Stirling Castle. James was almost a year old. The queen played happily with him, never guessing that this would be the last time she would ever see him.

As she and her servants rode back to Edinburgh they were stopped by Bothwell and 800 of his men who blocked the road. Bothwell took Mary away with him to Dunbar Castle. Hurriedly divorcing his wife, he married Mary just three months after the death of her husband – a death that most people believed had been masterminded by Bothwell himself.

Did Bothwell take Mary by force and make her marry him?

Bothwell stops Mary on the road from Edinburgh.

Mary's son, James, as a boy.

Or was she in love with him, and did she therefore go with him willingly? The evidence was unclear. Some believed that she was innocent; others believed she was a murderer's **accomplice**.

Mary and Bothwell were together for only a few weeks. The people were appalled at Bothwell's rise to power and saddened by the terrible fall from grace of their beautiful young queen. Protestant nobles were ready to join together against them both.

The darkest hour

Bothwell's army met the rebel lords at Carberry Hill on 15 June 1567. Mary was taken captive by the rebels and led back to Edinburgh. All the way she was taunted by jeering cries of 'Murderess' and shouts of 'Kill her!', 'Burn her!'

Tears ran down her face as she rode through the streets. That night she was imprisoned in a

Above *The castle on Lochleven where Mary was imprisoned.*

In June 1567 the rebel lords met Bothwell's army at Carberry Hill. Mary was captured by the rebels, and taken to Edinburgh.

house in Edinburgh. The next morning, broken and distraught, she cried pathetically for help from her window.

Later that night she was bundled unceremoniously on to a horse and made to ride through the darkness to a castle on an island in Lochleven, a lake 80 km north of Edinburgh. Unlike the island where she had stayed as a child, this was no refuge from danger: it was her prison. In total despair, Mary neither spoke nor ate for two weeks.

Bothwell was declared an outlaw. He could do nothing to rescue her and he fled abroad (where he died, insane, in a Danish prison eleven years later). Mary was forced to sign documents by which she gave up the Scottish crown to her son, James. Her half-brother, Moray, was to rule until James was of age.

On 29 July 1567, the thirteen-month-old King James VI of Scotland was crowned, while Mary wept on her island.

While Mary was imprisoned in Lochleven, her son, James, was crowned king of Scotland.

Escape to England

Mary was not without supporters, even on the island. With their loyal help she managed to escape after ten months, disguised by heavy cloaks and hiding in the bottom of a rowing boat.

Gathering an army of 5,000 men, she went to battle with Moray's smaller army at Langside. Her troops were defeated, however, and she had to flee to the south-west where Catholic support was strong. It

Above *Elizabeth I, queen of England, was Mary's cousin. When Mary turned to her, however, Elizabeth was unable, or unwilling, to offer any help.*

Right *Mary escaped from Lochleven Castle by boat under heavy disguise.*

was a frightful journey. For days Mary and her supporters rode hard, and (as she herself described it) had to 'sleep upon the ground and drink sour milk'.

At this point she made another terrible mistake. Despite the advice of friends, she chose to flee to England and seek the help of her cousin, Elizabeth. In May 1568, penniless and in disguise, Mary sailed in a fishing boat across the Solway Firth, landing in Cumberland. At once she wrote to Elizabeth, asking for her help.

But Elizabeth did not, could not, help. Elizabeth wished to protect Mary, for she was a cousin and a queen like herself, but she also feared her. For Mary was a Catholic. Any of Elizabeth's Catholic enemies could rally round Mary and if they did, it could prove very dangerous. Also, Mary was suspected of being a murderess, and she had married the man widely accepted as the murderer of her husband. So Elizabeth had to keep Mary under guard. Mary was taken to Carlisle Castle, no longer free to travel where she wished.

The Casket Letters

The Scots lords now produced a silver **casket**, containing what they said were letters from Mary to Bothwell, 'proving' that Mary had been in love with Bothwell and that they had together planned Darnley's murder. Elizabeth I set up a **Commission** to examine the accusations. Moray and others gave evidence to the Commission, but Mary was refused permission to do so.

It now seems clear that the letters were **forgeries**, created by the lords to discredit Mary and to save themselves from being charged with Darnley's murder.

With her usual skill, however, Elizabeth came down on neither side, saying that there was not enough evidence. Despite this, Mary was never allowed to leave England again. For the next nineteen years she was to be the prisoner of Elizabeth, although in all that time the two queens never met.

Mary was moved from castle to country house and back again. Several escapes were plotted, but none was successful. Plots were also hatched by Mary's supporters to release her and overthrow Elizabeth. It was one of these plots that finally destroyed Mary.

The present Chatsworth House in Derbyshire, built on the site of the house where Mary spent several years of her imprisonment.

The treacherous Scottish lords present the silver casket to Elizabeth I.

Fotheringhay

The years passed with Mary suffering from illness and increasing hopelessness as Elizabeth continued to put off making any decision about her. Her 'gaolers' grew ever more strict; her every move was watched.

   In 1586, Sir Anthony Babington (a wealthy Catholic) led a plot to overthrow Elizabeth with the help (he hoped) of the king of Spain. Babington wrote to Mary about his plan and she wrote back approving of it – not

Above *Mary's tomb in Westminster Abbey, in London.*

Below *Mary's execution warrant, signed by Elizabeth I in 1587.*

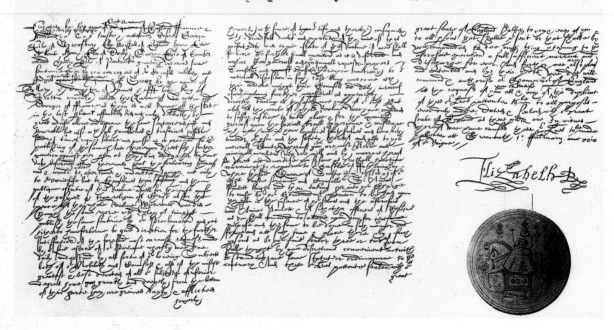

Warrant to Execute Mary Stuart, Queen of Scots, A.D. 1587.

Mary walked to the scaffold carrying her crucifix and Catholic prayer book.

knowing that every letter was intercepted by Elizabeth's spies.

Babington discovered he was in danger and attempted to escape, but he and his fellow conspirators were arrested and put to death. Mary was moved to Fortheringhay Castle in Northamptonshire.

There, on 15 October 1586, she was tried and found guilty of **treason**. It was obvious that the Commissioners had been convinced in advance of her guilt. It took only two days for them to condemn her. Yet still Elizabeth hesitated. Although she wished for an end to the threat to her crown, she did not want to take responsibility for the death of a kinswoman and a queen.

Eventually, on 1 February 1587, she signed Mary's death warrant. One week later, on 8 February, Mary was led into the hall at Fotheringhay. She knelt with her head on the block and the executioner's axe fell three times before her head was finally severed. In a life lived so close to violence, it was to be the final violent act.

Important dates

1542   8 December, Mary born.
14 December, death of her
father, James V.

1543   Henry VIII arranges marriage
between Mary and his son
Edward.
9 September, Mary crowned at
Stirling.

1547   The Battle of Pinkie Cleugh,
where English defeat Scots.

1548   Mary sails for France.

1558   Marries Francis, eldest son of
the French King. Elizabeth I
comes to the English throne.

1559   Becomes queen of France when
her husband is crowned
Francis II.

1560   Deaths of Mary's mother and
her husband.

1561   Returns to Scotland.

1565   29 July, marries Lord Darnley
at Holyrood.

1566   9 March, murder of David Riccio
at Holyrood.
19 June, birth of Mary's son
James.

1567   9–10 February, murder of
Darnley. Bothwell carries Mary
away to Dunbar.
15 May, marries Bothwell.
15 June, Mary and Bothwell
surrender to the Protestant
Lords at Carberry Hill.
17 June, taken to Lochleven.
24 July, forced to **abdicate** in
favour of her son James VI.
Moray becomes Regent

(Governor) of Scotland.

1568   She escapes from Lochleven.
13 May, is defeated by Moray's
forces at Langside.
16 May, flees to England.
October, Elizabeth sets up a
Commission to consider Mary's
part in the murder of Darnley.

1586   Mary arrested for her part in
the Babington Plot.
15–16 October, trial at
Fotheringhay Castle.

1587   8 February, Mary executed at
Fotheringhay.

1603   Death of Elizabeth I. As there is
no direct heir to the throne,
Mary's son, James VI of
Scotland, becomes King James I
of England when the two
countries are finally united.

1612   James I has his mother's body
removed to Westminster Abbey.

Glossary

Abdicate   To resign, especially to give up the throne of a country.
Accomplice   Someone who helps another person commit a crime.
Barbarism   Wild and lawless.
Casket   A small box for holding precious items, such as jewels.
Catholic   Belonging to the Roman Catholic Church, the religion headed by the Pope.
Commission   An official inquiry.
Forgery   A false document.
Heir to the throne   The person who is next in line to inherit the throne of a country.
Illegitimate   Illegal; born of parents not legally married.
Monarchy   System of government headed by one person, such as a king or queen, who inherits their title.
Protestant   Belonging to one of the churches that broke away from the Catholic Church in the sixteenth century.
Puritanical   Belonging to one of the extreme Protestant groups, with strict rules about how life should be lived.
Stuart   Mary's family name. This is the French spelling of the name; her Scots relatives (such as her half-brother James) spelled it Stewart.
Treason   Plotting to betray or overthrow a government or ruler.
Treaty   An agreement.
Tudor   Elizabeth I's family name.

Books to read

Mary Queen of Scots by Alan Bold (Wayland, 1977)
Mary Queen of Scots by Antonia Fraser (Panther, 1970)
Mary Queen of Scots by Jean Plaidy (Robert Hale Co., 1975)
Scotland under Mary Stuart by Madeleine Bingham (Allen & Unwin, 1971)
Queen Elizabeth I by Dorothy Turner (Wayland, 1987)

Index

Figures in **bold** refer to
illustrations

Babington, Sir
    Anthony 28–9
Battle of Langside 24,
    30
Battle of Pinkie Cleugh
    7, 30
Battle of Solway Moss 4
Boleyn, Anne 11
Bothwell, Earl of 18; **21**
    murder of Darnley
        19, 30
    marriage to Mary 20,
        30
    army defeated 22
    flees abroad 23
    letters from Mary 26

Carberry Hill 22, 30
Carlisle Castle 25
casket of letters 26
Catherine de Medici 12
Catholics 6, 11, 15, 24
Chatsworth **26**
Commission set up 26

Darnley, Lord Henry
    15, 18
    marriage to Mary 15,
        30; **15**
    murder of Riccio 16,
        17
    death 19, 30; **18–19**

Edward, Prince 6, 30; **7**
Elizabeth, Queen 13,
    25, 29; **24**

comes to throne
    10–11, 30
death 30

Fotheringhay Castle 29
France 8–9
Francis II of France 9,
    10, 11, 12, 30

Henry II of France 7, 11
Henry VII 11
Henry VIII 4, 6, 11, 30
Holyrood Palace,
    Edinburgh 14, 30; **14**

James I of England and
    VI of Scotland 30
James V of Scotland 4,
    30; **4**
James VI [Mary's son]
    20; **21**
    birth 16, 30
    crowned 23

Knox, John 14; **14**

Lochleven 23; **22**

Mary of Guise 4, 12; **4**
Mary Queen of Scots **4,
    5, 12, 22**
    birth 4, 30
    crowned Queen of
        Scotland 6, 30; **5**
    sails for France 7, 30;
        6
    at French court 8–9;
        8–9
    marriage to Francis
        10, 30; **10–11**
    Queen of France 11, 30
    death of husband 12, 30
    returns to Scotland
        13, 14, 30; **13**

marriage to Darnley
    15, 30; **15**
birth of son 16, 30
murder of Darnley
    19, 30
marriage to Bothwell
    20, 30
taken to Lochleven
    22–3; **23**
abdicates 23, 30
escapes from
    Lochleven 24, 30;
    24–5
army defeated 24, 30
flees to England 25,
    30
arrested 25, 30
letters to Bothwell
    26; **27**
prisoner 26, 28
Babington plot 28–9,
    30
trial 29, 30
executed 29, 30; **29**
tomb in Westminster
    Abbey 30; **28**
Moray, Earl of 12, 15,
    24, 26; **16**
    plotted against Mary
        16
    Regent 23, 30
    gave evidence to
        Commission 26

Protestants 16, 21

Riccio, David 16, 30; **17**
Ruthven, Lord 16

Scotland 6, 13
Stewart, James *see*
    Earl of Moray
Stirling Castle 6; **7**